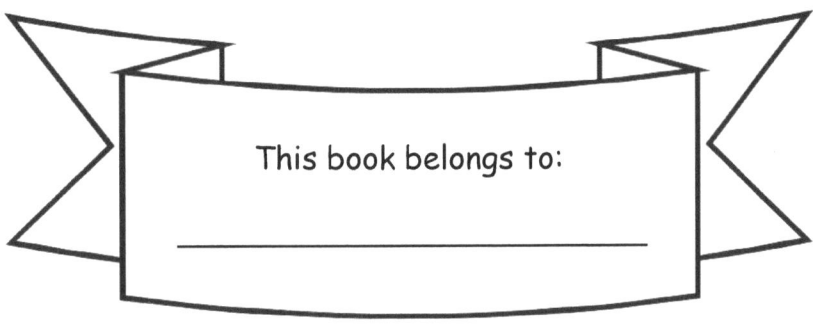

This book belongs to:

_____

This book is dedicated to
Jahmall Jr., Makaila Marie,
Tre'vyon, Ti'Ahna and Ta'Niah.

I am A Masterpiece: An Illustrated Poem

Written by Dr. Eniola Burton-Smith

Illustrated by Donald L. Hill, MBA
Edited by Shamirrah Hill, M.A.

Printed in the United States of America
ISBN-13: 978-1545161975 975

I am a masterpiece

I am unique

There is only one me

From the shape of my nose to the tips of my toes

I am the only me there will ever be

I am a masterpiece

Intelligent, astute, resourceful too

I strive to live in harmony and peace

My words ring true

I will be me, without doing harm to you

I am a masterpiece

Audacious, tenacious, and loquacious

Most closely mirroring bodacious

Never fearful or fallacious

I am a master of peace

Morally, ethically, responsible

Being accountable for my behavior

Living life, giving thanks to my Savior

Consciously doing the right thing

No matter what each day brings

I am a masterpiece

I am talented

Making use of my gift

Using words to uplift

Lend me your ear for these words you must hear

"Work smart in your classes. Bring joy to the masses."

I am a masterpiece

Beautiful in every hue

Celebrate me

I'll celebrate you

No limitations

No need to fit in

Don't you dare bend with every wind

Focus on what's inside your heart

Not what you or I can or cannot do

Share the gifts you have inside

Then you will become a masterpiece too

I am a masterpiece

Fearfully and wonderfully made

A work of art, a masterpiece

Rare like pearl-producing mollusks and clams

Yes, a masterpiece I am

Use this page to write all the wonderful words (adjectives) that describe you.

What does the word "masterpiece" mean?

What makes you a masterpiece? Begin with, "I am a masterpiece..." Then explain why.

_____

_____

_____

_____

_____

Find the words in the poem that you are not familiar with and write them on this page.

Write a letter to the author and illustrator on this page.

Teaching Page:

No individual or group is better than any other. As humans, we are all equal. Yet we are all unique, with our own individual skin.

Love the skin you are in. Whether you are black, white, purple, or green, don't search for reasons to be mean.

Learn to be in love with yourself.
Love your straight hair, your curly hair, your light skin, or your dark skin.

Love YOU!
Love ME!

Whether you are completely able or a little less able, love who you are.

Work to improve relationships.

All races, creeds, colors, and nations could learn a lesson about proper relations.

We are all beautiful in our own way. We are all individual works of art.

You are, we are, they are, and I am a **masterpiece!**

-Dr. E

About the Author:

Dr. Eniola TLB Smith is an educator, founder of "I Am a Masterpiece" youth programs, and developer of Triune International a non-profit community service corporation. She lives in St. Louis and dedicates her life to helping others live intentionally. Dr. Smith is a retired member of the Armed Forces of the United States, and she continues the mission by educating community members in the area of wellness with a focus in emotional and behavioral health. She is an advocate for survivors of assault and abuse, and strives to build safe, supportive environments where young people grow and learn with dignity. For program information contact Triuneinternational5@gmail.com

About the Illustrator:

Donald L. Hill, MBA is the founder of Donnie Graphics, an Arizona-based graphic design company that specializes in children's book illustrations and start-to-finish support for self-publishing authors. They serve as a one-stop-shop for illustrations, formatting and printing needs. Additionally, they create branding packages for authors and for entrepreneurs to help uplift and encourage them to "be all in" their full potential and passion. Donnie Graphics treats each client like a family member, giving 100% effort to create an original masterpiece each time. They're best known for their memorable top-quality designs and cost efficient prices. For more information visit Donnie Graphics at www.donniegraphics.com

*This book is recommended for grade levels 3-6

www.ingramcontent.com/pod-product-compliance
Lightning Source LLC
Chambersburg PA
CBHW060822290526
45792CB00005BB/1768